Shodh Yatra

Shodh Yatra

Research on Self (During Travel in Leh)

Dr. Palakh Jain

PARTRIDGE

To order additional copies of this book, contact
Partridge India
000 800 10062 62
orders.india@partridgepublishing.com

www.partridgepublishing.com/india

"When you know others, it is wisdom; if you know yourself, it is enlightenment"

Quoted in an article in Times of India (24th August 2008)

I read the above statement in newspaper as I sat in the flight from Delhi to Leh. I was fascinated by the quote and wrote it down. However, least did I know that I will experience in the next seven days what this quotation implied. Yes, to sum up my *"yatra"*, I should say that *I got to know myself.* In other words, I re-discovered myself all over again in a much better way.

What I experienced at different points of time is extremely difficult to pen down. It is something that I only I can experience – something beyond the feeling of achievement, beyond words, beyond the happiest moments!! It is a feeling which makes you feel great about yourself and one has to experience to know what exactly it is. May be it is a feeling which makes you realize your own hidden self and potential.

Surprisingly enough, even after experiencing something so unique, others cannot see what experience you have gone through. Nobody has told me till now that you have

changed. All they say is "**You have started smiling a lot**". I know I have but for a reason only known to myself.

The *"yatra"* provided me an opportunity to view the world in a different way. The view is not similar to the view we get when we sit in a car and things just pass by. However, it is how we view the world by **ruling it** i.e. the view we get from airplane!!

During the *yatra*, the learning happened from following four sources:

1. Listening to myself
2. Learning from each other
3. Learning from Nature
4. Learning from people

Though I learnt a lot from each of the four, however for the purpose of this report I am going to follow the following:

'Small minds talk about people
Mediocre minds talk about events
Great minds talk about ideas'

!

!

As it is impossible to incorporate everything in one report, the **primary focus of this report will be on the ideas that crossed my mind at various points in time**. I am focusing on ideas because I feel this learning is most concrete and robust. The other learnings will in some way or the other flow from this.

I took this course just because I like travelling. Before commencing the *yatra*, I was not expecting anything. I think that is the reason why I got the maximum out of it. I was not even aware of the underlying idea behind this course (I got to know that during the course).

> *Learning: To get the maximum, DO NOT EXPECT.*
> *Just do it properly with an open and cool and mind.*
> *The results will surprise you!!*

As the journey began, the flight went over the mountains. I was fascinated not so much by the scenic beauty but by the STABILITY depicted by the mountains. Seasons come and go, however, mountains stand tall even in most adverse conditions and that's the reason people admire the mountains.

> *Learning: Stand tall like a mountain even as seasons*
> *change. People will admire you for the same.*

On the first day of the trek, I realized that our life is nothing but something very similar to a trek. For understanding life, it is possible to draw parallel examples from the observations made during trekking. The following are some parallel examples I drew while walking on the very first day:

1. Initially, while walking I was looking down as the path was not even. I observed the stones and realized that **no two stones are alike**, the way no two people are alike. Hence, it is essential to observe people as you meet them in life. If you are not careful, you may miss the opportunity to appreciate the goodness of people as well as get hurt by others.

2. While walking (as in life), there were patches of greenery/ rocky mountains/ muddy path etc. I felt that the overall energy of the group increased or decreased as we crossed different areas. Very colorful patches gave us **positive energy** and the dull ones took the energy away from us. I could not understand what I could learn from it, however, the instructor mentioned about magnetic mountains when I shared this thing. I got an answer to a major question on the last day when I saw the magnetic

mountains. I will discuss the same in the last section of this report.

3. While walking, the speed used to decrease whenever we looked back. Hence, a lesson to be learnt was **NEVER LOOK BACK IN LIFE!!**

4. Depending too much on anyone (for crossing over rocks etc.) or on anything (stick) while walking (during life) breaks it. Hence, **TOO MUCH DEPENDENCE** should be avoided.

5. Every river/tough patch (obstacles in life) can be crossed by everyone. **Just realize your potential.**

6. I was tempted many times to just close my eyes while walking for a fraction of a second. I realize that in life, we do this mistake all the time i.e. **close eyes to the obvious things. Whenever we do so, we are bound to fall.**

Discussion on 'Voluntary Suffering'

The very first session on the above mentioned topic opened my eyes to a world I had been ignoring for past one year. *As the discussion went on, I stopped listening to what others were saying and heard my inner voice. I believe that surely was a moment of "<u>breakthrough</u>".* I cried after the discussion to realize how I had stopped undergoing voluntary suffering. It was for this reason; I had become what I never wanted to. It is impossible to define the amazing feeling I had after speaking my heart out to the professor. However, the broad impressions are as follows:

□ I should do what I BELIEVE in and persist doing the same

□ Making a choice is a challenge. It is a suffering!!

• Never stop making CHOICES. The day you stop undergoing the suffering, you loose your individuality.

'BREAKTHROUGH' for me was Re-INVENTING THE PAST and realizing that I LOVED undergoing voluntary suffering

MIXED FEELING: Moving on with the greatest sense of achievement and enlightenment ever attained, I found a new energy within me which is keeping me happy till date. I felt that my mind became all the more sharper and I was at peace with myself on one hand and was looking for perfection on the other. This mixed feeling is truly something that I want to live with forever.

CONRASTING EXPERIENCE: After drawing a few lessons from my journey, I decided to observe others. There were instances where I felt that no two people are alike and there were instances when I felt that the other person was a replica of what I was. Again, this contrasting experience helped me learn a lot as I moved on.

While descending from the mountain to the first village, I found trails already made for trekking. The majority of the *shodh yatris* followed the path already made. However, there were a very few who **made their own paths**. As they made their own paths, they followed it with much more enthusiasm even if it was tougher. On the other hand, the ones who were following the given path exhibited less zeal. After thinking about it, I concluded that the people who realized their own potential and capabilities were able to carve out their own paths. Also, they were not at all different from the others who did not make their own path.

> **Learning: Everyone has the potential and capability. As soon as we realize the same, we can carve out our own paths and follow it with a greater level of commitment and enthusiasm.**

however, I felt really small in front of the villagers who had realized their potential despite all the harsh conditions. *Do circumstances and conditions govern the way one makes his or her own path? Is it a determinant more important than realization of capabilities? I am still pondering over the same!!*

WHY DO WE FAIL TO SEE
THE LAP OF NATURE??

The next day while going to Shingor, I realized that the lap of Nature could be found anywhere. We often find people talking about going and resting in the lap of Nature. Least do we realize that there are elderly and experienced people around us for support. We always bypass them without realizing that to rest we do not need to come to mountains. The lap of Nature can be found in any urban city.

> **Learning: For relaxing in the lap of Nature, there is no need to go to the mountains. Just appreciate the presence of elderly people around you.**

The 4- hour solitude which revealed the essence of life to me

On 29th August we were asked to maintain a four hour silence (including visual silence). When I began, I was not really sure how would I pass time for such a long time without speaking. However, the eventual result was mind blowing. The overall experience not only helped me know myself better but I also learnt the essence of life. I feel what **I learnt was a *mantra* that can help me surmount the toughest problems in the easiest way possible.**

Before discussing what the end result was, I would like to discuss the sequence of things that happened in these four hours. I feel that each process helped me in understanding myself, my behavior, my attitude towards life etc.

COLLECTING STONES: When we were dispersed for the process of maintaining silence, most of the people grabbed a nice and comfortable corner for themselves. However, I preferred to walk. I started with collecting stones. As I kept on looking down to find the stones which fascinated me the most, I felt there were stones which attracted me but I bypassed them. I did not look back and moved on. I wondered how many times in life I must have turned myself into stone to people who needed me for one reason or the other. **I could not recall any instance however, I felt that at a subconscious level that I must have turned my back to people many times. I felt guilty but unfortunately I cannot heal the past. Hence, now a day I have started calling people more often. Also, I recently got gifts for my friends and sister after many years. Though no two stones and no two people are alike, I realized that I should not turn myself into a stone to people. I believe that I am on the right track now!! Also, I have become a much better and balanced person.**

TEXTURE OF STONE: I was amazed to see the contrasting change in the texture of any stone when it was wet and when it was dry. On one hand, the stone became extremely attractive,
vibrant and soothing when wet. On the other hand, it became very dull and lifeless when dry.

Learning: From the contrasting texture of a dry and wet stone, I deciphered the following-as an individual I would want to be a wet stone- oozing with life and energy! What can be the sources of the same? Just to name a few- constantly taking a dip in the pond of knowledge, satisfaction and complacency in all situations.

SEARCHING FOR A PLACE: For the initial one and a half hour, I walked. I searched for a place to sit. I could not find any! There were too many barriers when I tried to find my own place even at a place like this. Also, I was tempted all the time to go back to the places where other people were sitting specially the ones I knew. I also felt jealous of people who were sitting comfortably and even sleeping.

Impression: As a person, I face difficulty in finding a place for myself in this world- even at a place like Leh! There are barriers after every point. There are social barriers as I didn't have the courage to go far because I am a girl. There are other barriers also. For removing the same, I need to find answers and I am sure I will.

EUREKA!: Throughout the yatra I had tried my best not to take anyone's help in crossing any path. I succeeded most of the times. However, before starting the process of maintaining silence, I had taken help to come down from the mountain as the patch was quite rough. When I could not find a place to sit for almost two hours, the same path constantly nagged me. However, I could not muster the courage to take the same path without anyone's help. The thought of trying to climb the same rough patch crossed my numerous times. For two hours, I decided not to. However, after sometime, I did take the same path and that too without anybody's help!

EUREKA. I almost fell but I was elated when *I could do it all by myself* and there *I found my PLACE!!* And there I was sitting on a rock comfortably*. It was a great sense of achievement.*

> **Learning: Even I have the potential to take difficult path!!**

As I sat on the rock, even after achieving success of doing things without any help, I cried. I cried a lot. I do not know the reason though. Yes, I did feel a lot better. I even wrote a letter in which I described the situation in

life where I experienced the same feeling of being on the top of the world. I realized that I don't need to come in the lap of Nature to experience this amazing feeling, I know where I have to BE!!

LOOKING UP: As I drew parallel experiences from life with regard to the similarity in feelings at two different places, I decided to look up. Instead of looking at the stones, I thought of looking at the sky, the mountains etc.

I realized that as I was thinking all this while, the sunlight switched place from one peak of the mountain to the other. **I wondered that similar to the sunlight, seasons also change but we keep thinking in the same manner.** I tried to think if it is essential to change thinking with time. *Is it better to have a dynamic thinking or a static one?*

SITUATION 1	SITUATION 2
Changes in position of sunlight	Change in season
Shade and no shade	Snow and no snow

It is quite evident that situation 1 is of a **shorter span** whereas; the second situation is of a **longer duration.** Now the question remains how an individual should react in these two situations. What kind of a behavior will best fit each situation?

NOTICE HOW SUNLIGHT SWITCHES POSITION FROM ONE PEAK TO ANOTHER IN A DAY. SEASONS CHANGE ACROSS MONTHS. HOW SHOULD WE CHANGE????

The answer that I got from Nature in is line with the theory of Classical economists. Keynes' actions in short run may be harmful!!

ANSWER FROM NATURE:

Situation 1 i.e. the one of shorter duration, will just get over soon. Hence, one should <u>control reactions</u>.

The time duration is so short that we may regret later. **The lesser is the quantum of reaction in this situation, the lesser time it will take to pass.**

In situation 2 i.e. the situation characterized by a longer span, one needs to <u>stick by the decision</u> and <u>exhibit immense will power till the time season changes.</u> The rationale for this is quite evident from the very characteristic of this situation i.e. the long time span. If individuals change their stand it will just indicate a weak character. Further, changing the stand frequently may lead to an irreparable loss. **The strategy should be to make a CHOICE and stick by it even if involves "Voluntary Suffering". Take every pain and every challenge as it comes and SURPRISE YOURSELF!!**

The solution is in contrast to the underlying theory of Keynes. He argued that short run is important and action needs to be taken to correct things. The Classicals argue that in long run things will be fine. For the solution that I got from Nature, in the short run, one need not take any action and just control reactions.

As I got this beautiful answer from Nature, the following song came to my mind. It is a song from a hindi movie

"Hum Hai Rahi Pyar Ke" and it sums up my answer from Nature very beautifully:

"Kehti hain ye wadiyaan...badalega mausam
Na koi parwah hai, khushiyan ho ya gum
Aandhiyon ko jhelenge, dard saare lelenge...

Yun hi kat jayega safar saath chalne se
Ke manzil aayegi nazar saath chalne se"

AND I DECIDED TO MOVE WITHOUT FEAR!!

As the song came to my mind, I sang it in my mind many times and as I did I SMILED. Not only once but I kept on smiling. While smiling I actually felt the mountains, the air and every element of Nature smiling with me. I felt just GREAT!! I achieved more than what I had ever expected to.

After that I made a mud castle and destroyed it myself. I don't know why I did it. Hopefully, I will get an answer to that too.

Some other impressions which have stayed with me:

☐ SURPRISE YOURSELF
☐ A child observes, you do not teach.
☐ You know the answer yourself!
☐ KILL your DARLINGS

I do not think I would do justice if I conclude my report. For me the journey has begun....

Personal Strategy Report

Name: Dr. Palakh Jain   **Age**: 32 Years (16.03.1983)
Ultimate Objective: MOKSH

Current Lifetime

Mission: Contribute to the **bigger picture** by playing the assigned **role** perfectly.

Vision:
- To **align** thoughts, words and actions to achieve given goal at hand.
- To **achieve** the peak of sensuality & success in order to let go of lower vibrations and stay satisfied with the Self. This will ensure *balance* & *equanimity* of mind, body and soul.
- To embrace **death** with harmony, love and peace.

Present Mission: Realise hidden desire, potential and transform personality completely.

Values: Love thyself, Integrity, Excellence, Peace, Live & Let Live

Strengths	Weaknesses
- Guru, Right Knowledge - Ability to stay calm & focused in tough situations for longer durations - Ability to transform according to time - Eagerness to gain knowledge - Ability to clear clutter - At my best when I am submissive - Educational Qualification & successful career - Good Health	- Inability to distinguish between right & wrong - Inability to change as per situation, people and environment - Inability to see through things - Extreme mood swings
Opportunities	**Threats**
- Study Dharam - Gain knowledge of different fields and different geographical areas- Astrology, Feng Shui, Classical Music, Instrumental Music, Martial Arts - Limiting Beliefs - Explore life via traveling - Emotions	- Possibility of losing interest - Possibility of lack of guidance - Any unforeseen event

A special thanks to the wonderful mind behind the design of this life-changing experience called 'Shodh Yatra'.

Translation of Hindi Song

Assures the expansive valleys

Sunshine is around the corner

Felicity or gloom

Bear it with aplomb

Storm, pain all

When we journey hand in hand

Despondency turns to joy

The target is ahoy